Dearest Anna

Just a little book to say ~~~~
friendship, for the carin~~~~
the fun & laughter, for ~~~~ music & singing,
for the encouragement & prayers....

May our Lord continue to bless you & use you
on this new journey in Swindon. Hope your
course turns out to be everything you hope for —
enjoy your student days again!

Will miss you heaps so keep in touch!

Take care, my sister ♥

Love YSIC
Helen
x —— 24·08·04

GW00360531

tranquil thoughts
on friendship

David Baird

tranquil thoughts
on friendship

introduction

Don't walk in front of me; I may not follow.
Don't walk behind me; I may not lead.
Just walk beside me and be my friend.

Albert Camus

Friendship is a promise that one person makes to another with their whole heart. It is not a contract drawn up on paper but a solemn unseen vow that is constantly renewed with each meeting or reunion; a pledge to enjoy the good times together and to share the bad. A friendship is a bond that exists between two people who are not related or bound by any legal obligation. It is a reciprocal relationship based on levels of intimacy and commitment, and dependent upon these factors people will either be our casual friends, close friends, or our best friends.

Friendships pass through many different phases, from the excitement and discovery of new friendships, to the cementing process of support given in difficult times, to shared celebrations and happy landmarks, through to the deep, comfortable peace of an old friendship that nothing can shatter and that will be there till the end of life. There is room in our lives for all different types of friends, with whom we share different degrees of intimacy, and whom we see more or less frequently.

In an age when marriages frequently founder, jobs take us far from home, siblings are separated by oceans, and life seems to impose ever-greater pressures, friendships are the cornerstone of existence, bringing joy and sanity, wise advice, and unfailing loyalty. Each new friend who comes into our lives brings a special gift from which we can learn and grow. We should welcome them with open hearts and give our love as a gift in return, because without friendships in our lives we would be spiritually poorer, cast adrift without a lifebelt in a cold dark sea.

unlimited friendship

But what is a friend? A confidant?
A shoulder to cry on? An ear to listen?
A heart to feel?
Friend—so small a word,
So vast in feeling and filled with emotion.
Friend—a word that exudes love,
A simple word
That has no beginning and grows
Without end.

The house of friendship is solid, comforting and strong, built from honor and esteem on a foundation of trust and respect. Free from deceit, its rooms are generous and filled with courtesy and understanding. Its walls are lined with the warmth of human kindness. For its roof there is honesty, and through the windows of joy, there for all to see, is a beautiful garden of love where peace and harmony blossom and grow.

a home

9

let it blossom

It takes a lifetime to grow an old friend. Their shoulders have broadened to provide the support you need and have often been streaked by your tears. Their eyes have kept watch, and their hearts have skipped a thousand times. There has never been a problem you could not turn to them for help with. No argument has ever driven them away, only closer. While weaker friendships have come and gone, your closest friend has always been there in your heart, for every single living moment, and they will be at your side in your dying thoughts.

Best friends always expect to be there for each other.

being

Sometimes we allow ourselves to become so preoccupied that we don't even notice we have pushed friendship aside.

connected

We humans are fickle creatures. Constantly overwhelmed by the demands upon our time and pressures that sap our energy, we go spinning off through the most frantic moments of our life totally out of control. Yet it is precisely at these moments, when the elements are hostile, that we need our friends the most. They are the ones who can keep our feet on the ground and our heads clear. When our problems escalate to leave us feeling lonely and isolated, friends will help us to feel connected.

nothing can be hidden

A true friend is one who
Knows you as you truly are,
Understands where you've been,
Accepts who you've become,
And inspires you to grow.

footprints

Our lives are filled with acquaintances ...

Blurred figures who, for a moment, enter the protective sphere of our lives and then quickly leave without a trace. A friend, however short their visits and the lengths of time between them, changes us and we are never the same.

They leave their footprints behind. Inside. Not on the carpet but inside our hearts.

True friends leave their mark and change the landscape of our lives.

you can
always bank
on friendship

Is there a better investment than friendship?
A friend is always there for you when the chips
are down. They understand you and are prepared
to accept you as you are. In times of need they
are only a telephone call away, and regardless of
the problem you always know for sure that your
friend won't let you down. Friends are people to
laugh and joke with and are there beside you to
dry your tears. Whoever gives in the name of
friendship shall reap what they have spent.

"A friend is a gift you give yourself."

Robert Louis Stevenson

There is a particular feeling that comes over us when someone special enters our life and changes it forever—a feeling of shared understanding that makes our hearts smile. We feel encouraged, comforted and advised. Suddenly everything in our life is achieved with much greater ease. We have someone to cherish, and something to look forward to for as long as we live. We have been blessed with the greatest gift that is known to mankind. That gift is friendship.

a heart's
smile

"There can be no friendship without confidence, and no confidence without integrity."

Samuel Johnson

making friends

A friendship is something we make. It is a carefully honed masterpiece that will stand all the tests of time. There is no strict pattern or logic to people's choice of friends—they need not share the same political or religious outlook, one may possess wealth and the other not, they may be of opposite sexes, ages, or races—but place them together and chances are that before your very eyes they will begin to complete each other's sentences.

Ask a person who they
saw yesterday and they
might not remember.

But ask them who they shared their first box of crayons
with, who was in their gang, who were the cowboys
and who played the Indians, who wore their mother's

friendship leaves

high heels to clomp tea-party trays through the garden,
and they will immediately glow with affectionate
warmth and recall their nursery days and those extra-
special friends who will remain in their minds and
hearts forever. Despite all the years and distances that
have placed themselves between you, these childhood
friends would still, if you met them, be able to pick up
as if there had been no interruption at all.

a deep impression

twice the person we were

Having a best friend is like having a second you to call upon; someone who can hear and comment truthfully upon your deepest secrets and provide advice you value; someone from whom there is nothing to hide, in front of whom you are free to be yourself. They say that you can't pick your family but you can choose your friends. Your best friend is the most important choice you will ever make in life and you are theirs. They are as close, if not closer, than any relative. There is an open invitation in your life, and very few moments when they would not be welcomed.

sharing

Close friends have much in common, with shared feelings and outlooks, and they are more intimate and trustworthy than casual friends. They feel no discomfort in sharing confidences in the knowledge that what they tell each other will never be misused. There is an unspoken vow of honor and commitment between close friends, and they are the ones most likely to be seen at table amidst family and best friends.

nature's perfection

Look at a walnut tree. Is it not like a friendship? Born from the consent of a single seed and the willing soil, it weathers storms and seasons, rejoicing in the sunshine, puts down its roots, and grows to a magnificent height and an extraordinary age. The fruits of its efforts take many summers and as many winters to ripen. They cannot be rushed but can be anticipated with relish.

It is an example of the perfection of nature's love. Friendship, too, is the perfection of love: pure, exalted, proved by experience, the consent of hearts and minds withstanding the test of time.

Seasons will pass and leaves will fall but the trees stand firm.

soul friends

Show me the friends and
I shall know the person.

You can tell a lot about a person by the company they keep. If you desire to know a person, then study their friends. These are the people of choice—those the person chooses to spend time with, with whom they prefer to dine, share laughter and their companionship. Their friends are the mirrors of their souls, just as ours are reflections of us.

a good reason to celebrate

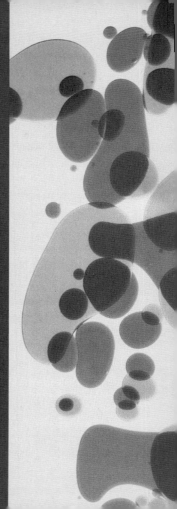

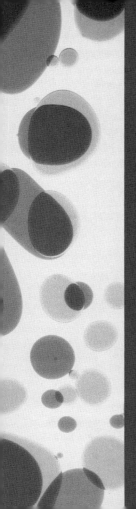

Why is it that we celebrate birthdays, wedding anniversaries and graduations, and yet there is no obvious date in the calendar year to celebrate one of the most important and significant relationships in our life? Friendship demands commitment on both parts and is deserving of its own ceremony. Why not dedicate a special day in each year to a commitment ceremony? It may simply entail stopping whatever else you are doing at a particular time to telephone each other from opposite ends of the world—just to say hello.

Sometimes we lose touch with friends. We move away. We change jobs. Our lives take unexpected turns.

But there is no time or distance that can keep true friends apart for they will always be in each other's hearts. They will always find each other again, no matter what the

friends find each other

odds against it, and when they do it will feel as if it were only yesterday when they last embraced.

emotional honesty

Why are we embarrassed by the intense emotions that a friendship can entail?

Why deny the depth of feeling we have towards another person just because they are not our mate, our intended, or our spouse? To suppress those feelings and deny ourselves the possibility of romantic friendship in our life is like preventing the sun from rising in the morning or holding back the tides—undesirable, and just as difficult. Only when we can acknowledge that friendship and romantic friendship are possibilities standing quite apart from the loving physical, intimate relationship of, say, marriage, will we remove the shackles from our heart.

What true friend would ever dream of steering you in the wrong direction? We should know that our friends only ever want the best for us and that they will always tell us the truth, even if what they say is something that we find hard to hear. No matter how difficult it may be for us to listen to their advice, it will be twice as difficult for them to give it and we should thank them for their honesty.

The wise advice of a good friend can often show us the right path to take when we can't see it for ourselves.

the moral bond

just good friends

What do we mean when we use the phrase "just friends?" Someone asks us about a person and we tell them "We're just good friends." Isn't that one of the most paradoxical things we could ever say when you consider that friendship is without doubt the most emotional, most intimate, and most intense relationship that anyone can possibly have?

Beware those who would sow seeds of doubt in your mind, for doubt is by far the swiftest of poisons if you wish to destroy a friendship. At first it irritates and then progressively the irritation turns to pain. Hurt, anger, and distrust form until doubt has seeped into every fiber of our being where it dissolves our friendship as effectively as ice melts on a hot stove.

sowing seeds

"Suspicion is the cancer of friendship."

Francesco Petrarch

person
to
person

Everyone has a particularly acute memory of that kind of aloneness associated with childhood—sitting on the swing with nobody to push you or getting a new football for Christmas and kicking it around the park alone. Even later in life the feeling persists. It might be working away from home and having to dine out alone, or being at the end of a crowded bar and overhearing conversations, stuck on the sidelines unable to participate. There are times when it seems that the whole world has a friend except you—then suddenly your ball comes rolling back and there's somebody who wants to play.

If you wish to see how much of an impact good news makes on someone, just watch the reaction of their closest friend.

glad tidings

While the receiver of the news is still reeling from the announcement, their friend will be whooping and cartwheeling down the street, unable to contain their joy.

perfect

It is fascinating to watch a group of friends relaxing together, taking time to bathe in the comfort of each other's company. It becomes rather like watching a well-rehearsed string quartet; so in tune are they with one another's wavelengths that the dynamics of

harmony

their laughter, their silences, and even the more somber moments, become like a curious form of music which is extremely pleasant to listen to.

Friends sing from the same song sheet and harmonize perfectly with each other.

no shame

Jealousy often drives mankind to extraordinary lengths and close relationships can become the target of venomous abuse. But however the world chooses to redefine the cherished friendships we develop in our lifetimes, our hearts will always know the truth. We have nothing to be ashamed of in our choice and love of friends.

friends become

"The greatest sweetener of human life is friendship."

Joseph Addison

entwined

Friends find us. They just seem to arrive. Someone appears in our life and our spirit and their spirit penetrate the outer, thick protective walls of character, age, sex, religion, and circumstances. Those souls entwine deep inside us, where love is formed. From that moment on we become as one; from a simple affinity, the meaning of our thoughts becomes enlarged and our life becomes free of deceit, leading us into the unknown where with no demands on either's part for power, physical pleasure, material gain, or oaths of duty.

each should know where they stand

No true friend will knowingly hurt or inconvenience the other. If there is something in your relationship which upsets you and they seem unbothered by it—say, for example, your friend is persistently late—then the time has come to speak up. Let your friend know the effect of their tardiness upon you and the strain it is placing on your relationship. Chances are they will mend their ways once they are aware of your feelings, but if they can't bring themselves to change, then perhaps it's time you recategorized your friendship.

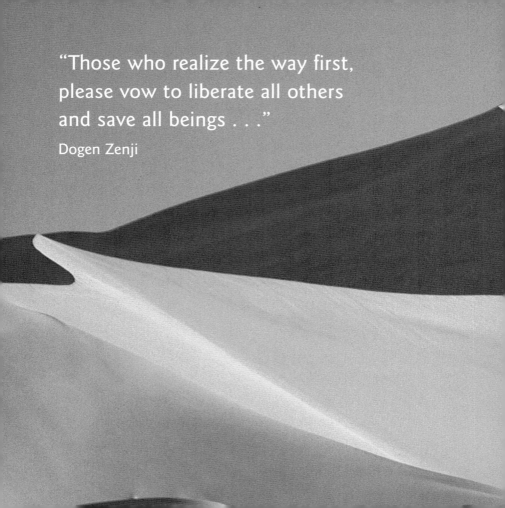

"Those who realize the way first, please vow to liberate all others and save all beings . . ."

Dogen Zenji

spiritual friendships

There is an ancient Zen saying that when the student is ready, the teacher appears. What will he or she look like? Look closer to home and to your own circle of friends. Is there amongst them one who is capable of opening your eyes to a vista beyond your own experience, and your mind to the possibilities that lie in an impossible situation? Such a friend can inspire us and shake us out of our daydreaming. Such a spiritual friend can guide us along the path that will awaken us to life's essential nature.

The notion of consecrated
friendships arose from the
sacred traditions and ancient
ceremonies of the North
American Indian tribes. Two
could become as one in
friendship through the
mingling of blood, achieved by
touching small, purposefully
induced wounds together
while swearing an oath of
undying allegiance to each
other in this life and the next.

blood brothers

intimacy

Life without intimacy is impossible. Friendship is the highest degree of intimacy anyone can aspire to achieve in a relationship. It goes beyond romantic love and endures all obstacles and the tests of time. A friend is there through thick and thin, and while friendship can sometimes develop into love, love when it fades rarely dissolves into pure friendship.

Friendship
is the most positive force
there is. Friends inspire each other and
feed off one another, encouraging, supporting,
and comforting the
other. Watch one friend
rowing in a race and the
other urging them on

encoura

from the bank; watch one performing a violin solo and
the other giving a standing ovation; one friend cooking
and the other delighting in the flavors. Friendships
like these are heaven sent—they demand
nothing difficult from us and they give
us everything in return.

gement

tokens of
friendship

When we are young children, we have little or perhaps no self-consciousness about expressing our affection for our friends. We spend hours with scissors, glue, and colored pencils making tokens of this affection to give to each other.

When we're a little older, we might even fashion friendship bracelets out of each other's hair so that we can feel ourselves almost woven into the very fabric of each other's lives, there to remain closely entwined as friends forever.

One moment we are all alone in a frosty gray world filled with shadows, and the next moment the sun is shining. Friendship is to humanity what the sunshine is to flowers, and there are flowers scattered all along life's pathway where there is a lasting friendship. Whenever we bring sunshine into the lives of others, we cannot keep it from brightening our own life too.

the sunshine of life

draw to the

Friendship is like a lightbulb to a moth. Where two friends gather their brightness is such that they soon attract others to draw closer to them. Suddenly there is a circle and everybody wants to be there, to please and be pleased by all around them. Where such a circle of

light of friendship

friends gather, laughter usually forms and is so infectious that it spreads beyond their own group to momentarily touch the lives of onlookers and passers-by, reaffirming for them, too, that friendship isn't all about being serious—it can also just be good fun.

friends
in their
best light

Friends are the candles that shine in our darkest night. They are the beacons on the hilltops, the lighthouses that guide us safely back to port. They are the welcoming glow of the front door light that lets you know you have arrived—home.

Friends light up our darkest hours and glow with pride at our successes.

a world
of friendship

What can be more fulfilling than making friends around the world, and keeping the friendships going with letters and e-mails? Even if we are unable to get to our friend's land in person, our ongoing correspondence provides us with a vital glimpse of their way of life. Given the opportunities the internet provides for making new friends, we can all have a global experience without leaving the comfort of our chairs. We can breakfast with our family, lunch with friends in Bali, take afternoon tea with friends in Rio, and be back in time for supper with news to share.

Even the most dangerous
or tedious of journeys can
become an adventure in
the company of a friend.

journey's end

With a friend by your side things don't just pass by—they are
observed and discussed, pointed out or discovered. The path to the
top of the mountain doesn't feel quite as steep and long train tunnels
don't appear quite as threatening as they would alone. Arrival is a
joint achievement and a cause for celebration, and suddenly we find
that instead of dreading the next commute to work we are looking
forward to it, and to being with that traveling companion again.

Friendship has a curious nature. Often it evades those who consciously seek it. Instead it comes to those who don't long for it at all, and usually when they least expect it. You can't go out and buy it.

the curious love of

Friendship is like all the other aesthetic joys and pleasures in life—art, music, and literature. When it is gratuitous, there is no obligation on either part. It becomes beautiful and free. But the moment we try to place a price tag on it, it takes on a whole different meaning. Keep your heart open and friendship will feel free to enter.

friends

trust and belief

"The glory of friendship is
not in the outstretched hand,
nor the kindly smile, nor the
joy of companionship; it is
in the spiritual inspiration
that comes to one when
he discovers that someone
else believes in him and is
willing to trust him."

Ralph Waldo Emerson

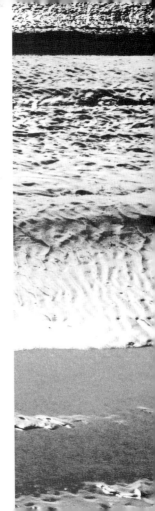

the river

If life were a river that flowed in two directions and two friends were caught in opposite currents ...

No matter how many changes in direction as they went with the flow, each friend would, for the other, always remain just around the next bend.

first visit home

Remember the first time you took your new friend home to meet your family? The house was clean that day and there were no chips in the crockery or mismatched forks upon the table. The air of expectation was a curious mixture of pleasure and anxiety. When the friend arrived, there was an atmosphere almost akin to fear and you watched those familiar to you suddenly become more graceful and your friend on best behavior.

It feels critically important that those we are close to like and approve of each other.

Neither side wished to corrupt the humanity of the situation with vulgarity or ignorance, and each wished fervently to make a good impression on the other.

Children have an uncanny way of inventing an imaginary friend who faithfully plays with them and accompanies them in times of need. Sometimes these friends are quite ordinary and love baked beans like you or I. At other times they might be pink unicorns who eat only orchids. Just because most of us are not privileged enough to see these fantasy friends, it does not give us the right to deny them their existence. Many of us would benefit from traveling on the subway or walking home on a cold, dark, rainy night in the company of a six-foot yellow rabbit named Harvey. But in the main, through our lack of imagination and in our rush to grow up, we have become compelled to travel alone.

everywhere

whispers

Having close friends not only offers us a place to pour our hearts out when we feel down, but also gives us the freedom to air our grievances, to challenge authority, or just be outrageous, without reproach, and without censorship. Where but in friendship can people openly share their antisocial ideas, vent their treasonous feelings, or divulge their deepest secrets? A friend is one who will listen as we express our worst fears, deepest anxieties, hates, distrusts, and weaknesses. They won't sit in blind judgment or nod in sycophantic agreement.

friendship is a

comforting smile

Overseas travel can produce feelings of anxiety that literally overwhelm us. It can be terrifying arriving in a foreign land and stepping out into a sea of unfamiliar faces. But imagine seeing one smiling, welcoming face standing out from the rest of the crowd. It immediately becomes recognizable as the face of your friend and suddenly everything is okay. All the anxiety gives way to another feeling, a good feeling that has no equal—Friendship.

home
comforts

"It is comforting when one has a sorrow to lie in the warmth of one's bed and there, abandoning all effort and all resistance, to bury even one's head under the cover, giving one's self up to it completely, moaning like branches in the autumn wind. But there is still a better bed, full of divine odors. It is our sweet, our profound, our impenetrable friendship."

Marcel Proust

vintage
friendships

Friendship is the wine of life. Born of a
memorable vintage and bottled with
affection, it lies in the protective cellar of
our heart, there to age and mellow to
perfection. And along life's way, we'll pop a
cork or two together and remember the early
days, our vines heavy with the fruits of our
friendship, and we'll toast the unknown future.
There will be other sun-kissed vintages along
the way for us to harvest and bottle, adding
a variety of new bouquets and always the
clinking sound of glasses that have been filled
to the brim with loving friendship.

just

Friendship goes beyond the height of a person, or the fact that they wear braces, have a stammer, or freckles, or no hair. None of these detract from their great sense of humor. They may be gangly and awkward, outspoken or absolutely silent, far too slow, wheelchair-bound or impossible to keep up with—but that doesn't matter one bit. They are our friends and that's the most important thing. We love them as they are, just as they love us. Despite the fact that they might not be as good at something as somebody else, they positively shine in their own special way.

sow and you shall reap

If you wish to harvest friendship, then sow courtesy. There is nothing like friendship to abate misery and intensify our happy times. Friendship divides our grief between two and doubles our joy. So plant a friend's kindness and you will gather a friend's love.

a library of friends

What can compare with the feeling of intense excitement that rises in us when we make a new friend? It is an exquisite pleasure that reaffirms our

faith in human nature and fills us with optimism for the future. A new friend is like beginning to read a new book, with discoveries to be made with every turn of the page, each new chapter. Our oldest friends are like favorite novels that we return to often and with great fondness throughout our lives. Both are deserving of a place of honor on the shelves of our library.

fidelity

There is only one creature in
this world that loves us more
than we love ourselves, and that
is our pet. Man's best friend is
said to be the dog, and it's easy to
see why when you watch a dog
greeting or defending its master or
mistress, or lying at their feet, and the
hours spent in tail-wagging, face-licking
frolics. What could be a clearer sign of true
friendship than a mouse that has been
allowed to travel in its owner's pocket?

Friends have a unique way of finding each other with very little initial effort on anyone's part. It's a mystery, but it happens. Watch children at play in a large group and you'll see that they avoid those they dislike until two eventually choose each other and a new friendship is born. They will not wish to be parted and will long to meet each other again and again. They'll need help to arrange those meetings until they are old enough to get together independently; meanwhile it is up to their guardians to invest time and effort on their behalf to establish a friendship that may last two lifetimes.

Young friends prefer to be with each other all the time and no one else will do.

Casual friends are more than
acquaintances or just people
we happen to know.

company

A casual friend is someone that we
would certainly go out of our way for—
but probably not out on a limb. We
will have some things in common
with them and share in a fondness for
certain activities—walks in the country,
gardening, riding, or films. They may
receive a seasonal greetings card but
probably not a seasonal invitation.

together

The deep peace of friendship

The very best kind of friend of all is the friend you can sit beside on the water's edge for the span of an entire night and never ever say a word. Just sit and gaze, watch the sky, collect shooting stars, listen to night sounds, then part feeling as though you have had a wonderful, meaningful conversation.

Published by MQ Publications Limited
12 The Ivories
6–8 Northampton Street
London N1 2HY
Tel: +44 (0)20 7359 2244 / Fax: +44 (0)20 7359 1616
e-mail: mail@mqpublications.com
website: www.mqpublications.com

Text © 2003 David Baird
Cover image: Grace Carlon, Flowers & Foliage
Interior images: © Digital Vision

ISBN: 1-84072-466-8

10 9 8 7 6 5 4 3 2 1

Printed in China

Note on the CD

The music that accompanies this book has been specially commissioned from composer David Baird. Trained in music and drama in Wales, and on the staff of the Welsh National Opera & Drama company, David has composed many soundtracks for both the theater and radio.

The CD can be played quietly through headphones while relaxing or meditating on the text. Alternatively, lie on the floor between two speakers placed at equal distances from you. Try to center your thoughts, and allow the soundtrack to wash over you and strip away the distracting layers of the outside world.